YOU ASKED, I LISTENED.

For years, people have been telling me to write down all of the crazy and wacky shit that comes out of my mouth, and I never thought anyone would care enough to buy an entire book with all of that nonsense, but here we are. So **THANK YOU!** You're why I'm putting together a list of these words and sayings. This is a collection of 15 years' worth of stuff I've been jotting down in the Notes app on my phone. Funny things I've said, even funnier things I've heard, I write it all down for later. After starting this fun little project, I've numbered the list, and it's over 6,000 pieces. Who in the hell wants to read all of that? No one. So, I've plucked out a handful of my favorites for you. This is only the beginning!

If any of these goofy words or sayings belong to you or someone you know, keep your eyes on your own paper, Mary. They're just words strung together, and there's no way for me to fact-check every line. I'm not Fox News. Oh, wait...they don't fact check either. Also, if you know some of these sayings, just enjoy them again, some people have never heard them before. I'm also not looking for any feedback or criticism, I get enough of that from my psychiatrist.

I've put each of these sayings and jokes on their own page so that you can rip it out and put it on your wall or carry it around with you if you love it. You could even hand one to someone to really get your point across. And honestly, I wouldn't blame you if you did. They're all genius.

LET'S GO!

To everyone who has felt like they were never good enough or didn't fit in, this one is for you! I wish I had a book like this growing up that I could use as a reference!

Use the stuff in this book as tools to verbally eviscerate those people who want to mess with you, or if you just want a funny comeback. Or if you're bored and just flipping through this at your friend's house while you're taking a shit. I don't care what you're doing...

Just enjoy!

THAT'S
A LOT
TO THINK ABOUT!

HEAVENS TO BETSY!

GOOD HEAVENS!

WHO'S TO SAY?!

MOVE IT, DICKNOSE.

I'll be
the judge
of that.

WELL MAYBE
iT BEARS
REPEATING!

Listen up, Little Susie sour crotch!

DON'T GET YOUR GRANNY PANTIES IN A WAD!

I WOULD RATHER RUN NAKED THROUGH THE JUNGLE WITH A BAND OF PIGMIES.

Yeah, hilarious.
Thanks for sharing.

WHO'S MY FAVORITE LITTLE APPLE JOLLY RANCHER?!

YOUR BELLY BUTTON LOOKS LIKE A COIN SLOT.

HEY
SQUASH
BLOSSOM!

YOU NEVER DO MISS AN OPPORTUNITY, DO YOU?

I've eaten enough
to cripple a pig.

...which I am.

WATCH IT, BUCKET MOUTH.

I think we should just make a couple of margaritas, put our feet up on the table, and clip our toenails.

Long tongue Larry, go ahead and give me a kiss!

It all comes back to roost!

I FORGOT

I HAD A

HEADACHE.

I am at MAX CAPACE.

YOU BET YOUR BOTTOM DOLLAR!

Que Pasa, Mang?!

WELL ISN'T THAT JUST THE BEE'S KNEES!

Let's make sure we're on the same page about your whereabouts on January 6th...

HE LOOKS LIKE A PEDOPHILIC BORDER COYOTE.

HE TOLD ME THAT HE'S AN EVANGELIST AND A MAGICIAN...

I'LL LET YOU HAVE THIS ONE...YOU GET SATISFACTION FROM A MAN SO INFREQUENTLY.

I'M JUST A BOY WITH NO ARMS TRYING TO MAKE MY BED.

HER HOBBIES INCLUDE CRYING AND DOUCHING.

I JUST LEARNED ANCESTRY.COM ISN'T THE BEST PLACE TO FIND A DATE.

I WAS JUST BEING THE WORLD'S SILLIEST GOOSE!

YOU HAVE THE CONFIDENCE OF A MUCH TALLER PERSON.

As a former 3
year old,
I understand
the frustration.

I'M HOT ENOUGH TO FUCK BUT TOO UGLY TO DATE.

I DON'T KNOW WHAT ALL THE HUBBUB IS ABOUT!

LOOK AT THAT MOIST LITTLE OYSTER!

STOP!
HAMMER TOE!

It looks like you've been mauled by an ostrich!

SHE SNORES LIKE THE TEXAS CHAINSAW MASSACRE.

Good work, Agent Low.

These charlatans need to be taken off the fucking streets.

NOT MY CIRCUS, NOT MY MONKEYS.

I DON'T KNOW IF YOU'RE BUSY, BUT I JUST DOUCHED...

GIVE ME THE PICKLED PIGS FEET AND CHEESECAKE.

THE PARAMEDICS STORMED MY HOUSE LIKE THE CAPITOL.

HE SMELLS LIKE FERRETS AND LIMA BEANS.

No cancer has ever looked at my brain and thought "What a ripe harvest!"

Your sock is untied!

"O"
AS in
OVERCOOKED.

You just go
back to gnawing
on rat pellets.

What do you mean you don't believe in Valentine's Day...? It's on the calendar.

I MADE iT,
BUT SAFEWAY
PACKAGED iT
FOR ME.

I can cook Minute Rice in 57 seconds.

She told me my socks were like "Warm, slick, fuckin' bitch bags."

What do you think she meant by that?

I'VE BEEN TAGGED LIKE A NATIONAL GEOGRAPHIC WILDEBEEST!!!

I HAVE A FETISH FOR TOES AND HORSERADISH.

I cum so much,
I could shampoo
a buffalo.

I WISH I WAS
AS THIN AS
HER HAIR.

HE'S DUMBER THAN PIG TRACKS.

This is my place... 49 square feet of luxury!

"LET'S GO TO STARBUCKS?" WHAT'S A FRAPPUCCINO GOING TO LEAD TO? A PIGGYBACK RIDE? NO!

Alright, I'm going to make like parents and split!

MY LITTLE MUNCHKIN FROM MY MUFFIN!

I BLOCKED HIM LIKE MY ARTERIES.

IT'S A THANKLESS JOB, BUT I'VE GOT A LOT OF KARMA TO BURN OFF.

GOOD TALK, LET'S HAVE IT AGAIN...

DOES ANYONE HERE KNOW THE FIRST SIGNS OF SYPHILIS?

UNLIKE AMERICA, LET'S ALL KEEP MOVING FORWARD.

WHY DO YOU CARE?

DOES HE HAVE BLACKMAIL PHOTOS OF THE STATION MANAGER FUCKING A GOAT?

CHECK OUT THOSE MUD HOOKS!

SHE HAS THE IQ OF a BUCKET OF MUSTarD!

GOOD!!!
That bitch probably choked on her whistle.

"UNCLE" USED TO BE MY SAFE-WORD WITH MY EX-BOYFRIEND.

I DON'T KNOW...
HIS FORESKIN
LOOKED LIKE
PENCIL SHAVINGS
OR TORTELLINI.
IT MADE ME
REALLY UNEASY.

Isn't there a Chia Pet somewhere that needs your attention?

FUNNY...

WHEN IS YOUR NETFLIX SPECIAL COMING OUT?

CANCELING THIS SUBSCRIPTION BECAUSE I'M DONE WITH HIS ISSUES.

I WOULD LOVE TO, BUT I'M DAIRY-FREE.

I'M NOT MEAN, I'M JUST CRUSTY.

CHECK OUT HER LITTLE WHISKER BISCUIT!

WHITE PEOPLE AGE LIKE MILK!

I'D LOVE TO,
BUT I'M
HEADED TO
MY SLOUCH
AND MOPE
SEMINAR.

THAT'S VARSITY LEVEL NONSENSE!

HE'S GOT THOSE BIG ASS TORPEDO NIPPLES FLAPPIN' ABOUT!

His first shift at Walmart selling Maxi Pads will wake him up!

BRAD'S MEAT KITCHEN, WHAT'S YOUR BEEF?

I'M NOT RUDE, YOU'RE JUST A PUSSY.

I'M AWAKE TOO MUCH.
I'M SO MUCH LESS
TROUBLE WHEN
I'M ASLEEP.

I HAVE THE PERSONALITY FOR DIVORCE.

I RESPECT YOUR COMMITMENT TO THIS DRAMATIC PAUSE...

If I can't eat it or drink it, don't buy it for me.

WOW!

YOUR POWERS OF OBSERVATION NEVER CEASE TO AMAZE ME...

I'D RATHER STAY HOME AND DE-CLAW MY CAT.

HE HAS A GROSS LITTLE PONYTAIL SHORTER THAN FEBRUARY.

If there's one thing I can't stand, it's YOU!

I don't want you to treat me any differently.

This is who I am now.

I DON'T CARE
"HOW YOU ARE."

I WANT TO KNOW YOUR
MOTHER'S MAIDEN
NAME OR THE STREET
YOU GREW UP ON.

I'D RATHER SEE
A VIDEO OF YOU
READING OUT LOUD
SO I KNOW YOU'RE
NOT FUCKING
DUMB.

WHO iS "WE?!"

DO YOU HAVE A POCKET FULL OF WORMS?

IT LOOKS LIKE HE COMBED HIS HAIR WITH AN ELECTRIC TOOTHBRUSH.

SHE'S LIKE A VACUUM WITH NIPPLES!

I'M JUST DONE WITH HIS GAMES. I AM NOT THE GAME SHOW NETWORK.

THERE IT WAS...

A BASEBALL DIAMOND FULL OF RED PUBIC HAIR AND A SARDINE GASPING FOR AIR.

EXTREMELY

UNNECESSARY

CLARIFICATION

THERE...

JUST TELL HIM YOU'RE A THIEF AND A CARTOGRAPHER.

THAT'LL BE THE LAST TIME YOU HEAR FROM HIM, I PROMISE.

JUST SAY THIS -

"YEAH THAT HAPPENED TO MY SISTER, BEFORE SHE WAS INSTITUTIONALIZED."

HER MOUTH
IS LIKE a
QUILTED
QUICKER
PICKER
UPPER!

Our first stop is the geriatric ward, where Lorena sings a piano ballad of "This house is on fire, let the mother fucker burn."

AT 34 YEARS OLD, I'VE SMELLED ALL THERE IS TO SMELL.

OR SO I THOUGHT...

ONE TIME, I GOT AN "ADVENTURES OF MARY-KATE & ASHLEY" VHS TAPE IN THE MAIL AND I BLACKED OUT.

HER ASS LOOKS LIKE A NURSING HOME MUFFIN.

THERE'S NO NEED TO OPEN YOUR EYES, YOU DIDN'T WITNESS A CRIME.

HE'S DUMB BUT PRETTY...

A LETHAL COMBINATION.

SAD LITTLE SUSIE'S OUT FOR A STROLL AS A SINGLE.

No no no,

He's on payroll...

She's on Parole.

That makes my butt itch.

YEAH, I'VE ALWAYS SAID THAT.

CALL FEMA, THIS IS A DISASTER!

DIDN'T I JUST WISH YOU HAPPY BIRTHDAY LAST YEAR?

WITH HER INTELLIGENCE LEVEL, SHE CAN OPERATE ANY SLURPEE MACHINE IN TOWN.

Yeah, sure...
I'll do that
when Stevie
Wonder hits a
home run.

THE TWINKLE IN HIS
EYES IS ACTUALLY
THE SUN SHINING
BETWEEN HIS EARS.

MY HOOKUPS ARE SO BAD....THEY COME IN, SEE MY BODY, AND INSTEAD OF BANGING ME, THEY BANG A U-TURN.

ASTROLOGY...

I DON'T BELIEVE IN IT. BUT THAT'S TYPICAL OF A

PISCES!

NO, BECAUSE THAT'S LIKE ASKING FORREST GUMP TO PERFORM BRAIN SURGERY.

I'VE SEEN MORE CEILINGS THAN MICHELANGELO.

YOU'RE NOT PRETTY ENOUGH TO BE THIS STUPID.

I got on the scale this morning and it said "Come back when you're alone."

OH THAT REMINDS ME...
I GOTTA PICK UP MORE
SALT FOR THAT WOUND.

I JUST KNOW THE FUTURE OF MEDICAL SCIENCE DEPENDS ON YOU KNOWING MY EMPLOYER.

I'm having the best week ever! I deserve a segment on VH1.

I COULD ROLLERBLADE
DOWN VENICE BEACH
AND FLIP MY HAIR
TO THAT SHIT
ALL DAY LONG!

YOU KNOW YOU'RE GETTING OLD WHEN YOU CAN'T PROPERLY PRONOUNCE "TURNT UP" LIKE THE COOL KIDS, DESPITE EXTENSIVE PRACTICE.

DO YOU GUYS TAKE BATHS TOGETHER?

My idea of partying is like 3 toppings on a frozen yogurt!

JUST LET THEM SWEATER PUPPIES HANG.

He had the personality of a surgical mask and a buffet napkin.

My loins are vibrating like a tuning fork.

Oh you got "Swag"? Don't forget to put that on your Burger King application.

I CAN'T BELIEVE I'VE SPOKEN TO TWO PARTIES IN CHARGE OF THE MUSIC PIPING THROUGH THIS ESTABLISHMENT AND NO ONE HAS PLAYED MY SONG YET. WHAT GIVES?

The ecology is going to Thank You when some coyote is choking on that shit.

THAT'S A WHOLE 'NOTHER KETTLE OF CRAWDADS, AS THEY SAY. THEY'RE SLIPPERY LITTLE BASTARDS THAT SQUIRM INTO PLACES THEY SHOULDN'T. MUCH LIKE THE HOOKWORM!

I'M WATCHING MY WEIGHT AND THINKING ABOUT YOU NAKED IS AN APPETITE SUPPRESSANT.

MY NAME IS BRAD, BUT YOU CAN CALL ME BRADLEY FOR SHORT!

THAT MIGHT JUST RUFFLE MY CORNHOLE AND STRAIGHTEN MY PUBIC HAIRS.

NOTHING LIKE A LA-Z-BOY TO ITCH THE OLD CHILI RING!

THERE'S MY FAVORITE LITTLE GUATEMALAN LOVE LIZARD!

Just look at that Purse-Dragging sissy!

This is the guy you use to let crunch your monkey?!

Aaaaand

SCENE!

That's it! That's all she wrote.

Not really, but this is all I'm giving you now. There are another 5,000 of these sitting in my Notes app, and by the time I'm ready to write another book, I'm sure I'll have a few hundred new things written down, ready to grace the pages of Volume Two!

From the bottom of my heart, seriously,
THANK YOU!

I'm just a 30-something-year-old guy living in LA, trying to pay my bills and feed my 4 Cavalier King Charles Spaniels!

Thank you for buying this silly, self-published book I wrote and designed and for reading through the nonsense. Hopefully you had a good laugh at some point. These gems are yours for the taking. Use them as you see fit. But I'm not taking ANY of the blame for what happens.

Follow me on Instagram to keep up with Volume Two updates! Feel free to message me with any of your gems, and I will gladly include some of them in the next book!

With love,
@bradlow (<--- That's my Instagram!)

Made in the USA
Las Vegas, NV
03 April 2024

88168855R00174